PENGUIN BOOKS

THE SITA COLOURING BOOK

Devdutt Pattanaik is the author of over twenty-five books and 500 articles on the relevance of mythology in modern times. Trained in medicine (MBBS from Grant Medical College, Mumbai University), he worked in the healthcare and pharmaceutical industries for fifteen years before devoting all his time to his passion for decoding beliefs of all cultures, modern and ancient, located beneath the veneer of rationality. To know more, visit devdutt.com

D0746499

DEVDUTT PATTANAIK

THE SITA COLOURING BOOK

PENGUIN BOOKS

An imprint of Penguin Random House

PENGUIN BOOKS

USA | Canada | UK | Ireland | Australia
New Zealand | India | South Africa | China

Penguin Books is part of the Penguin Random House group of companies
whose addresses can be found at global.penguinrandomhouse.com

Published by Penguin Random House India Pvt. Ltd
4th Floor, Capital Tower 1, MG Road,
Gurugram 122 002, Haryana, India

First published by Penguin Books India 2016

Copyright © Devdutt Pattanaik 2016

10 9 8 7 6 5 4 3 2

ISBN 9780143426462

Typeset in Adobe Garamond Pro by Manipal Digital Systems, Manipal
Printed at Replika Press Pvt. Ltd, India

www.penguin.co.in

Publisher's Note

The Sita Colouring Book brings together 108 images from Devdutt Pattanaik's bestselling retelling of the Ramayana, for you to colour in using your imagination.

The great epic unfolds through these illustrations; for the full story, we would like to direct readers to Devdutt's *Sita*, to which this is a companion volume.

The pages of *The Sita Colouring Book* can be coloured in using colour pencils and crayons.

Also available is *The Jaya Colouring Book*, featuring Devdutt's illustrations from *Jaya*, his bestselling retelling of the Mahabharata.

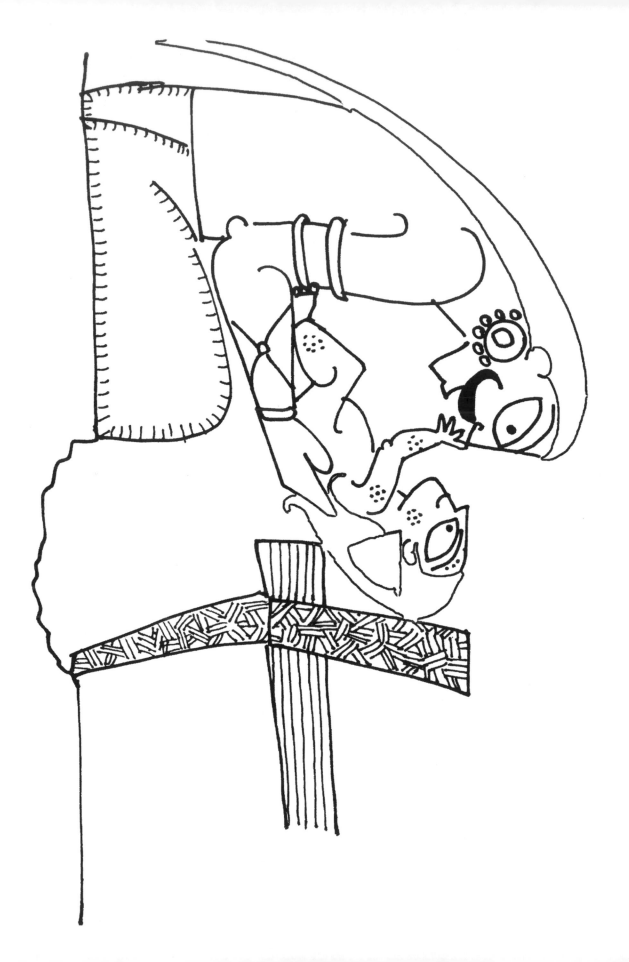

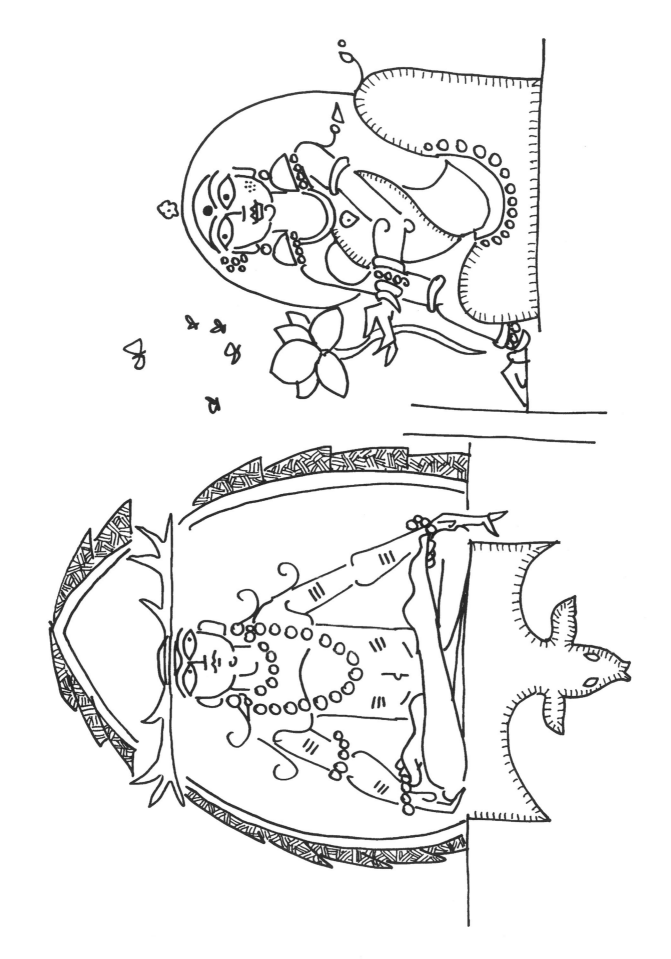

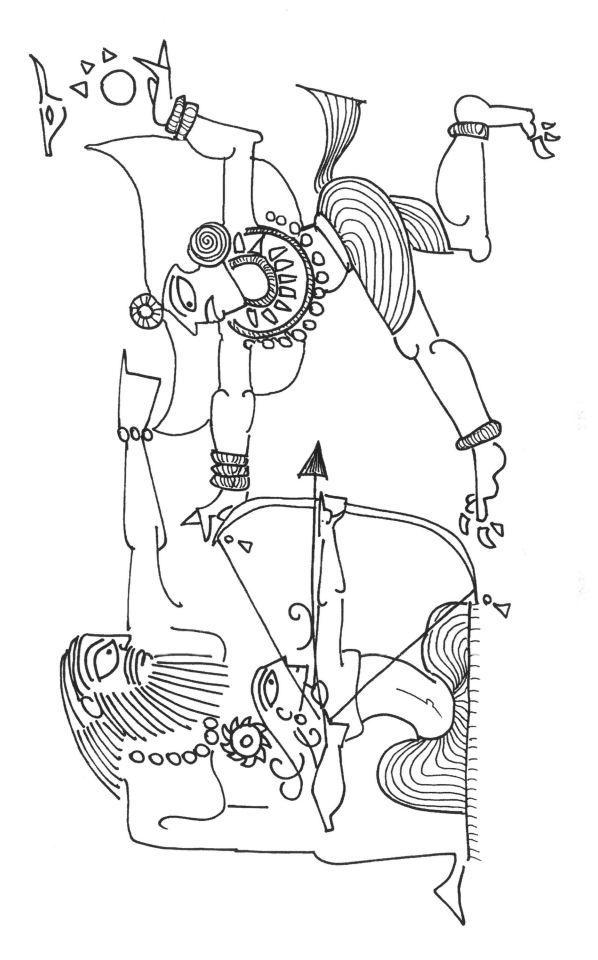

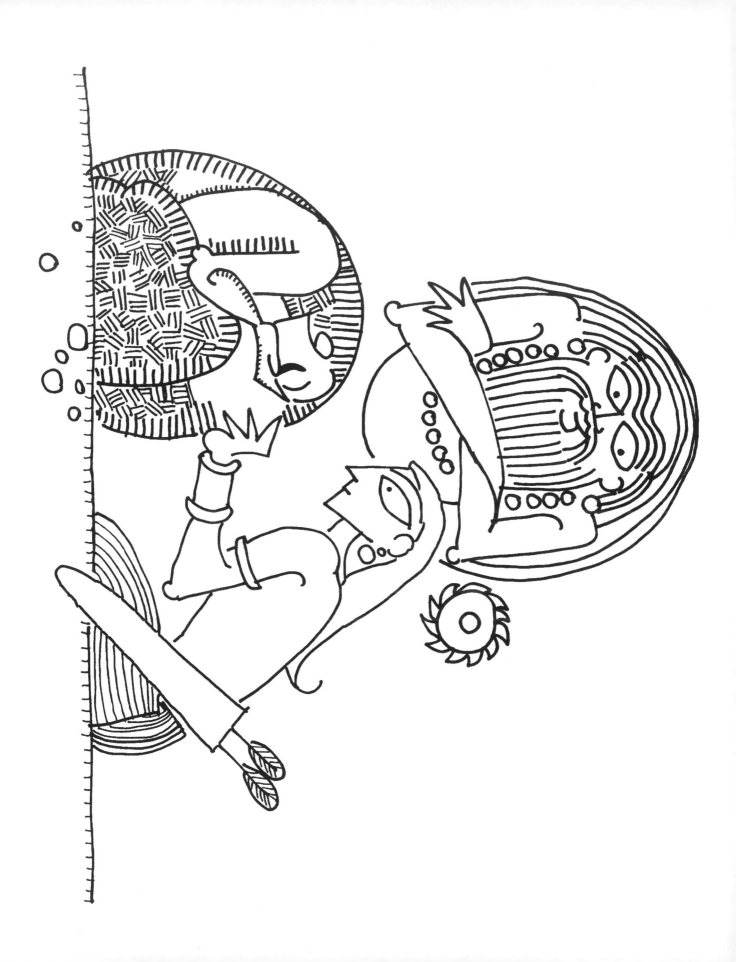

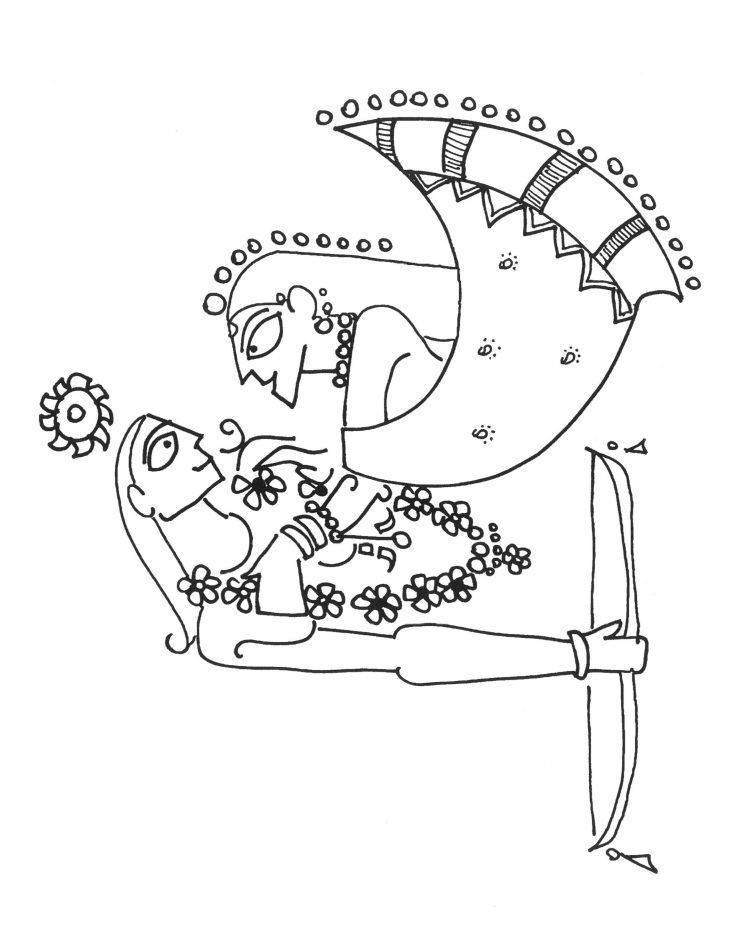

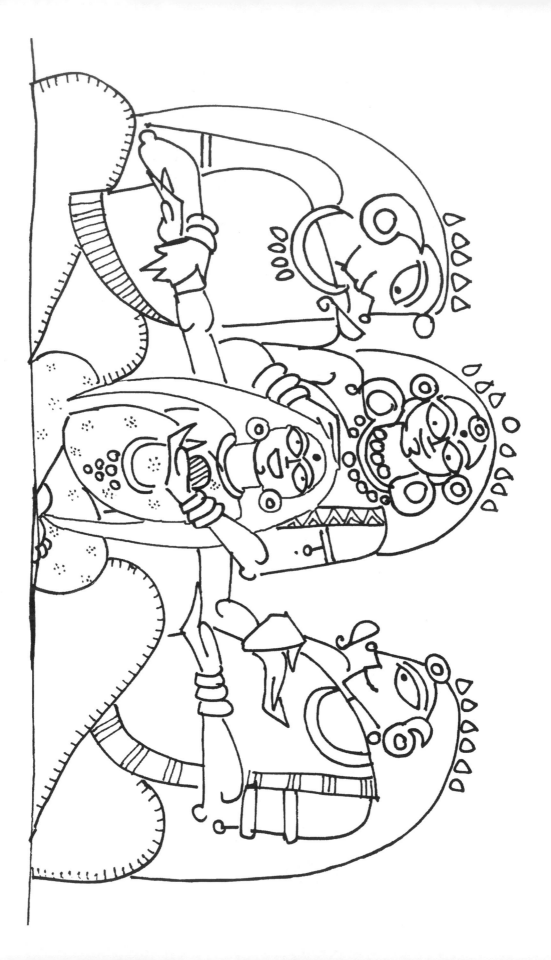

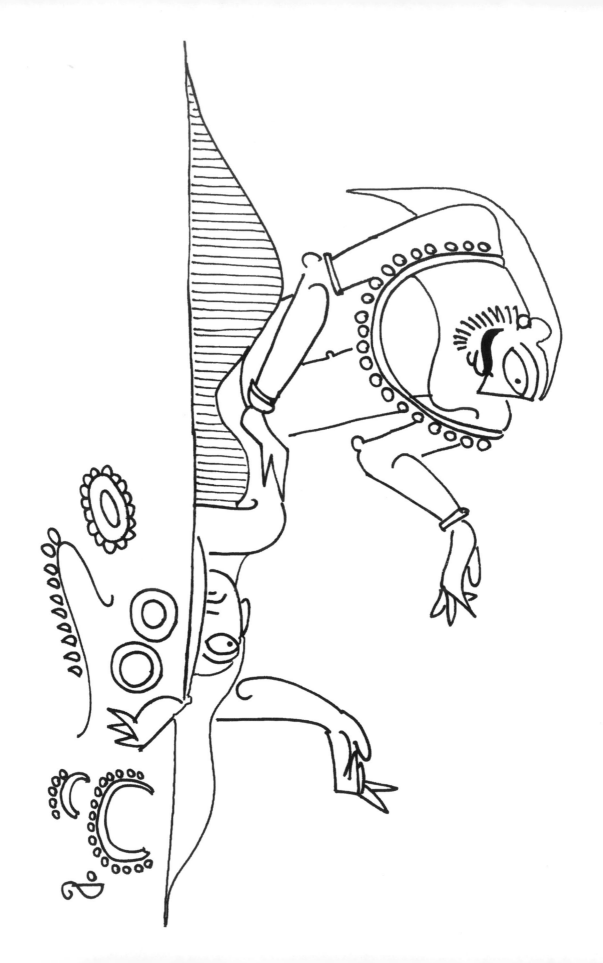

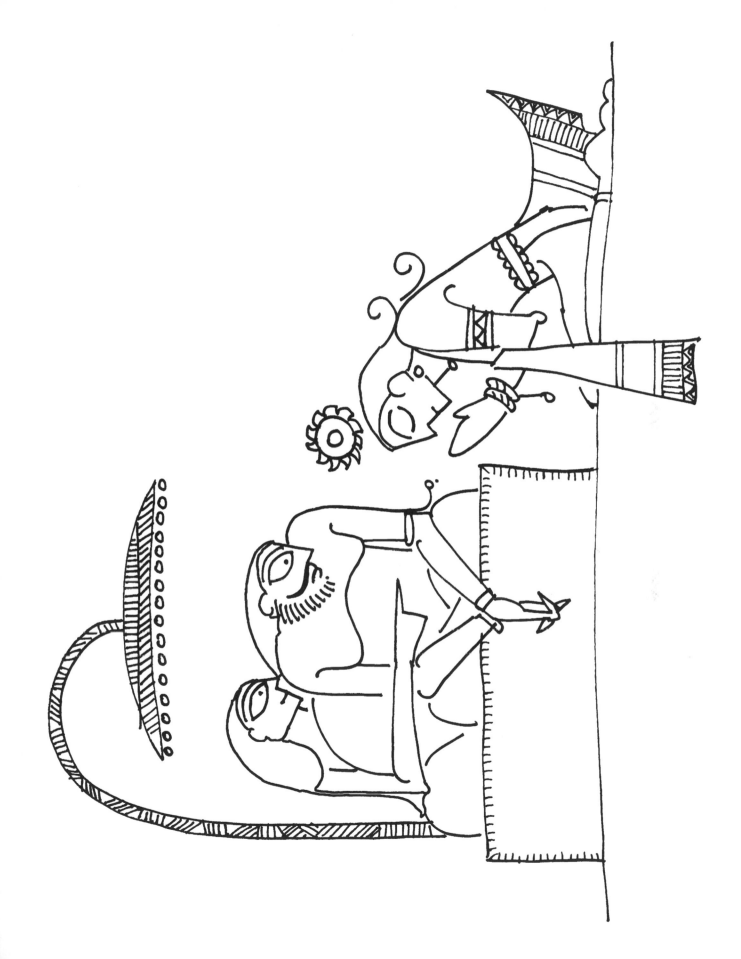

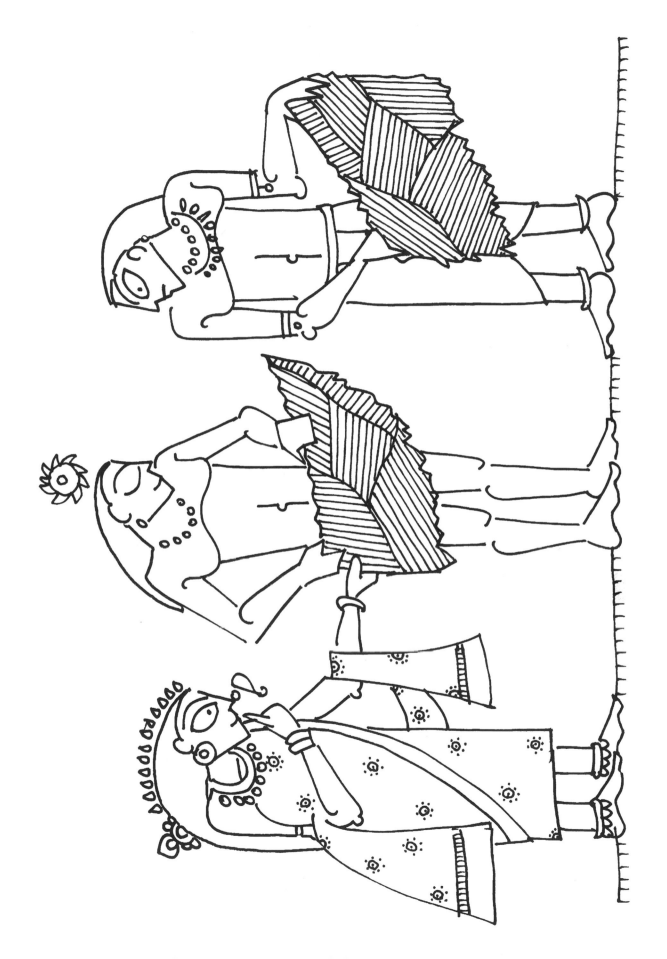

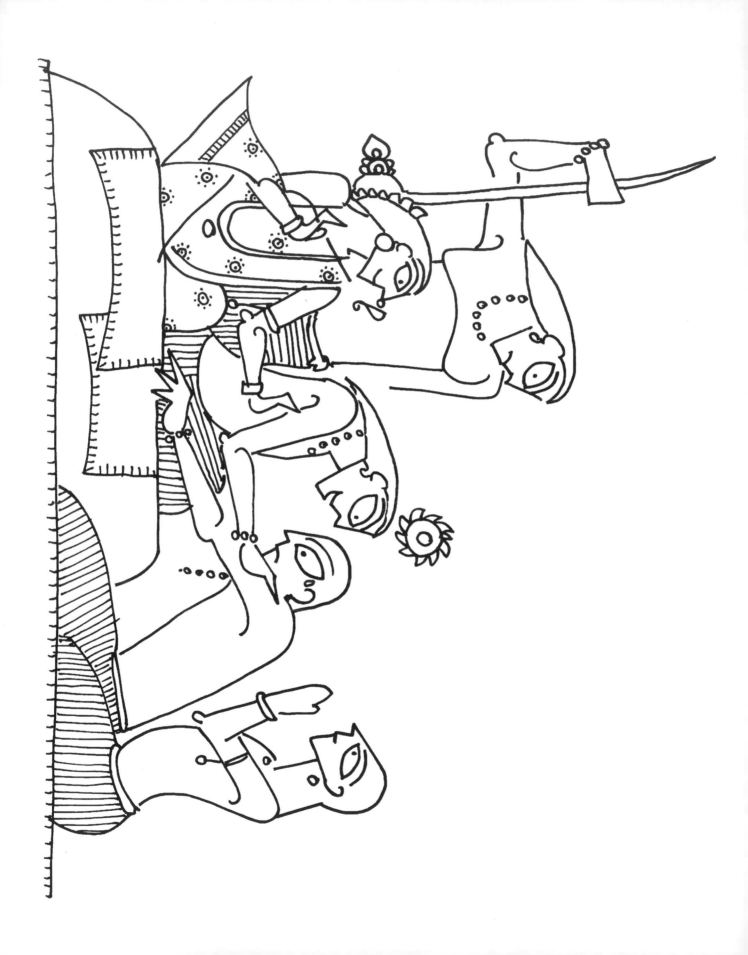

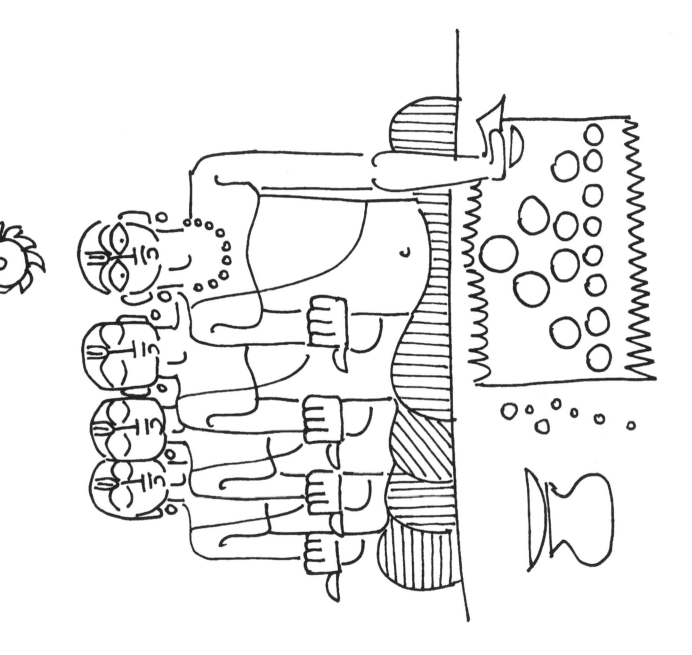

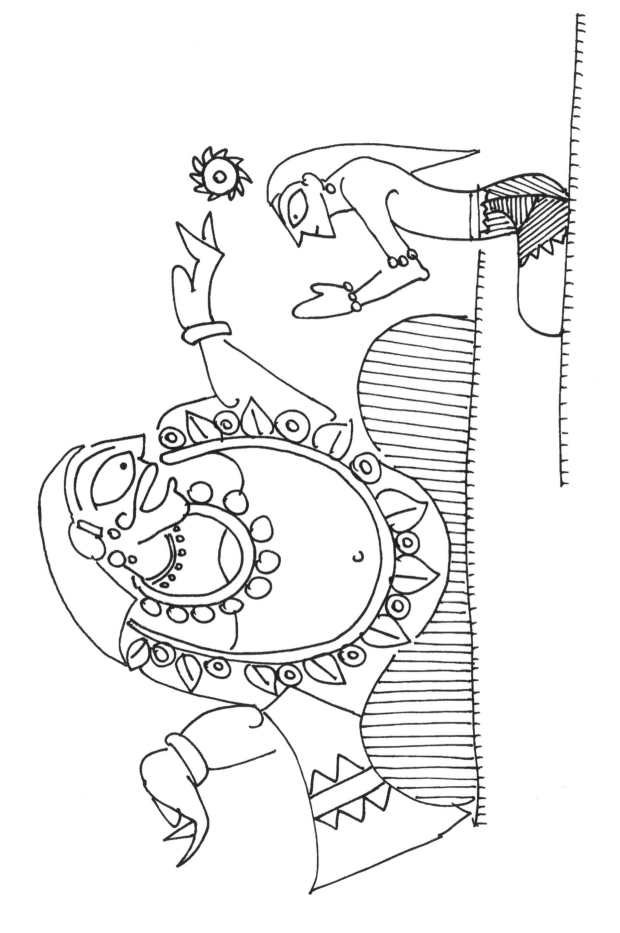

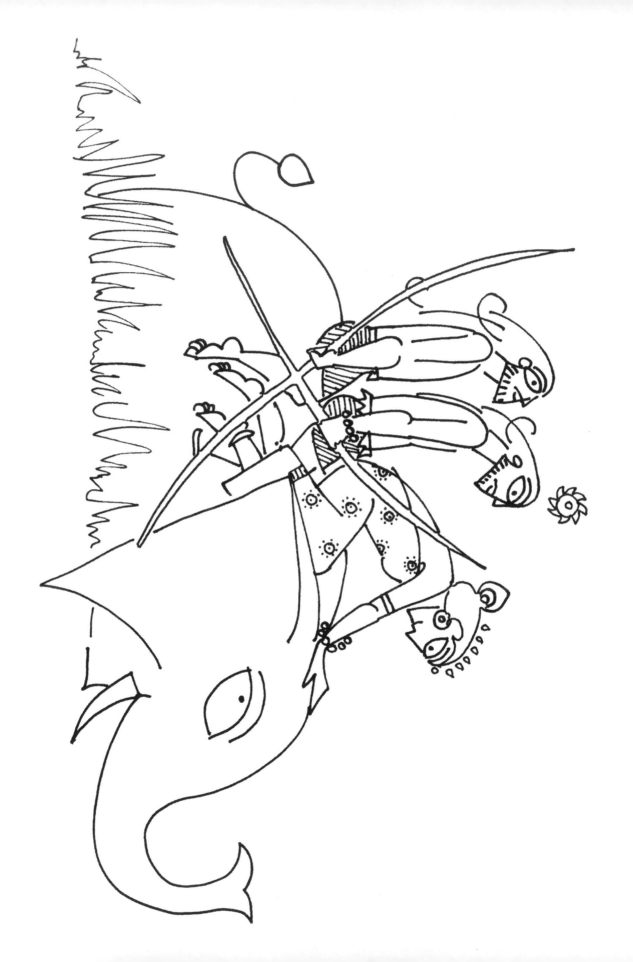

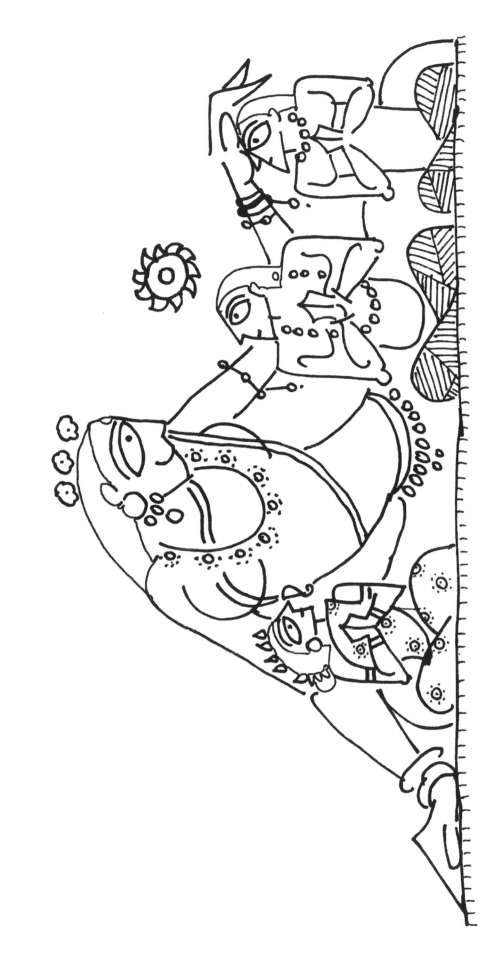

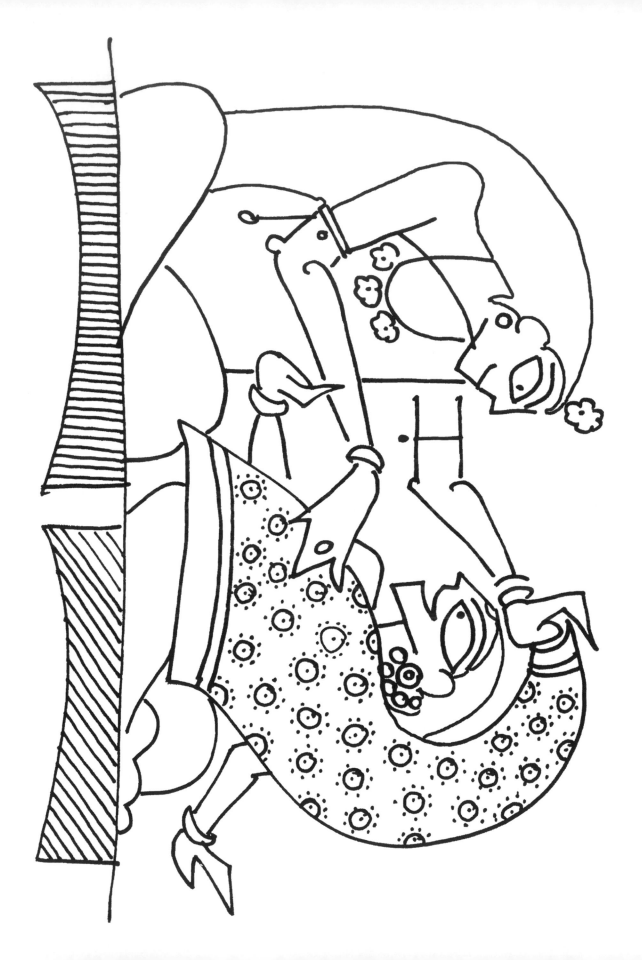

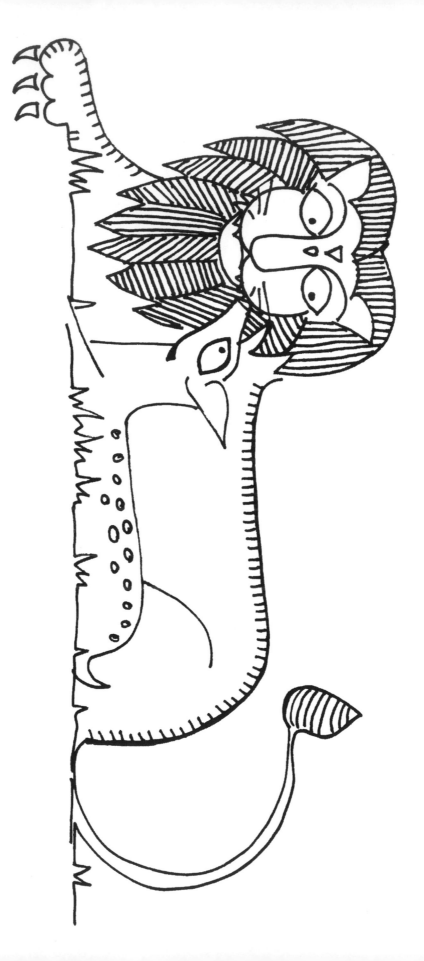

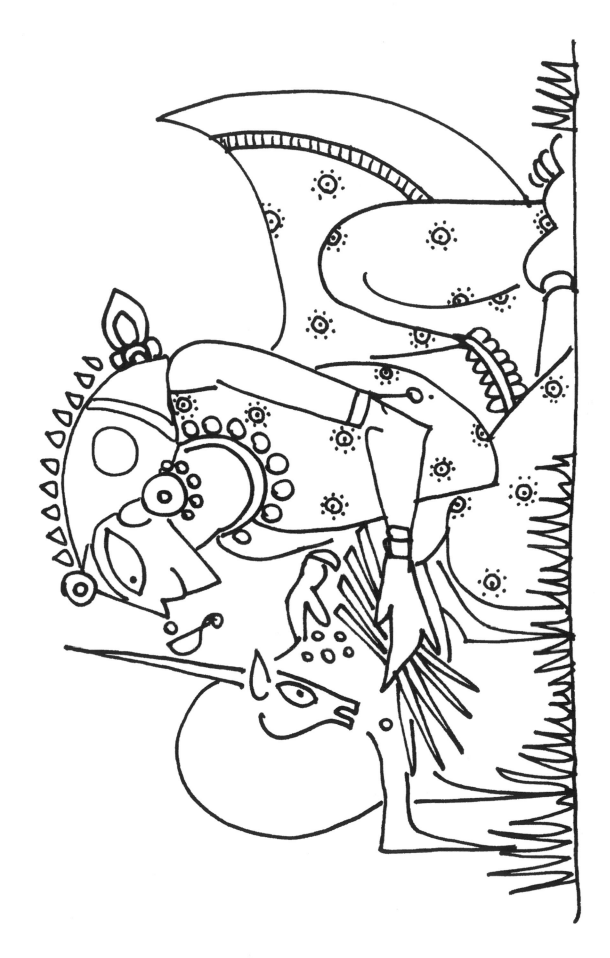

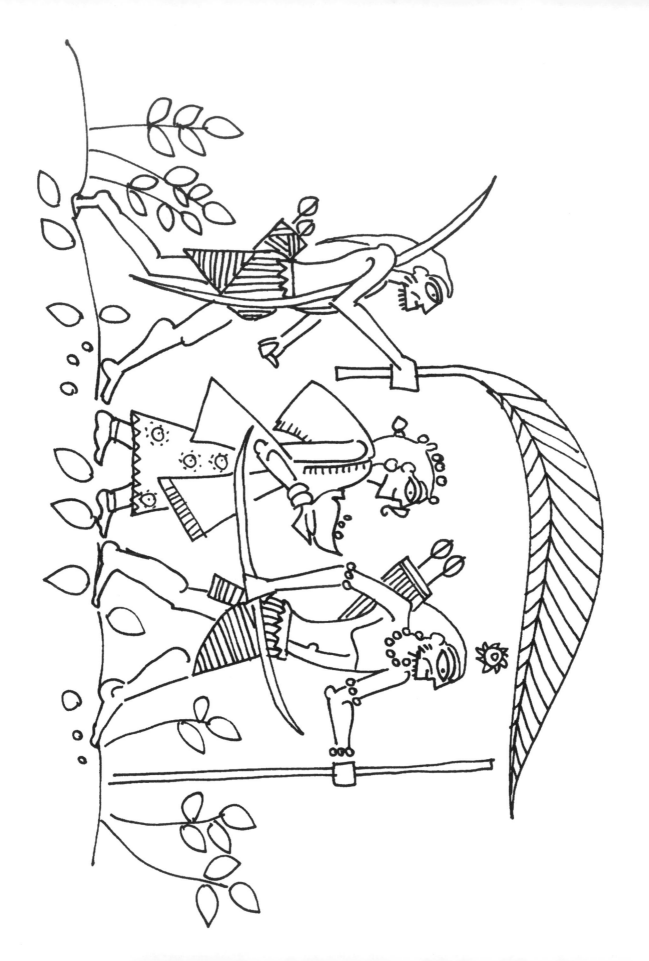

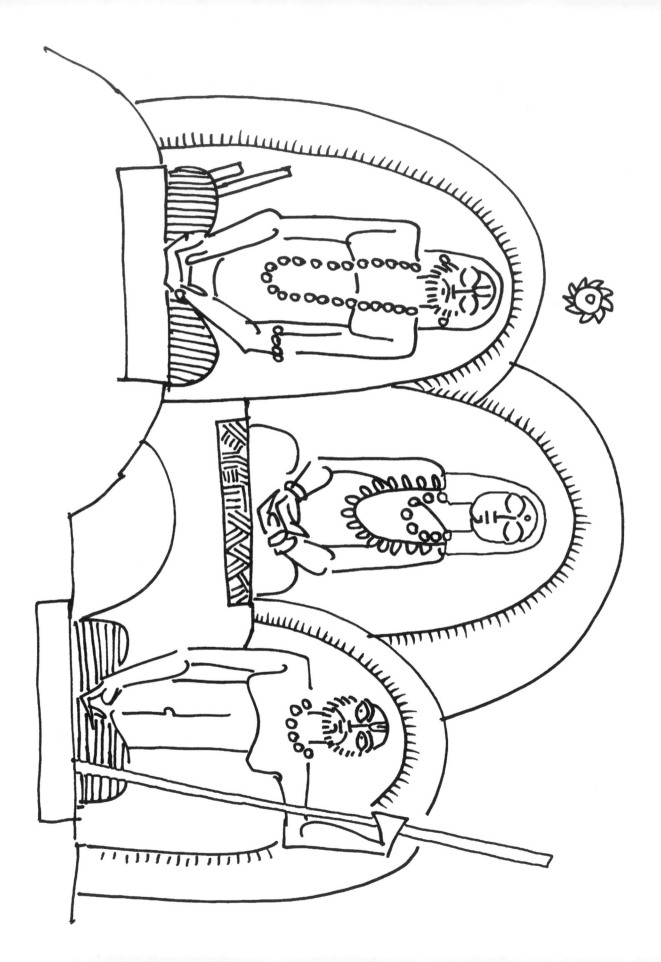

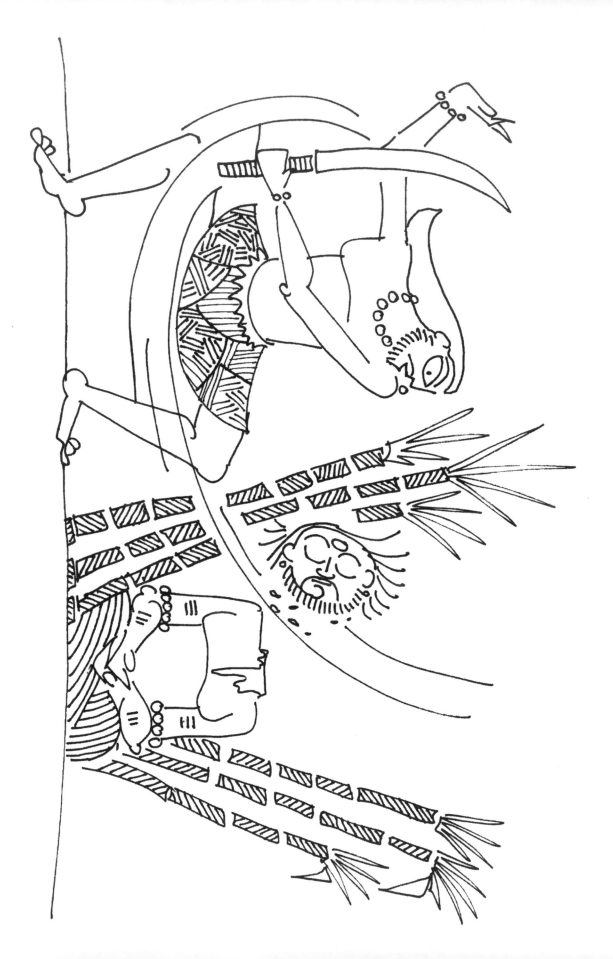

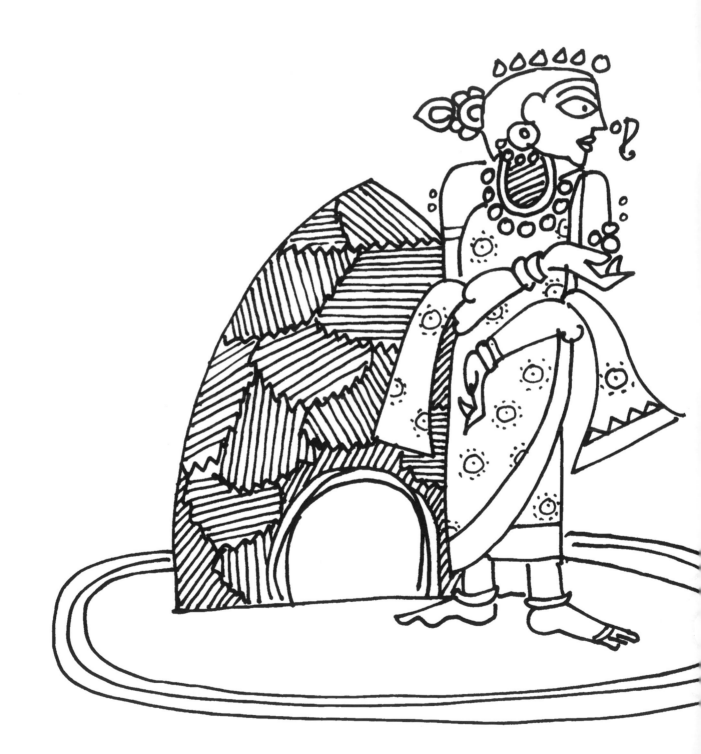

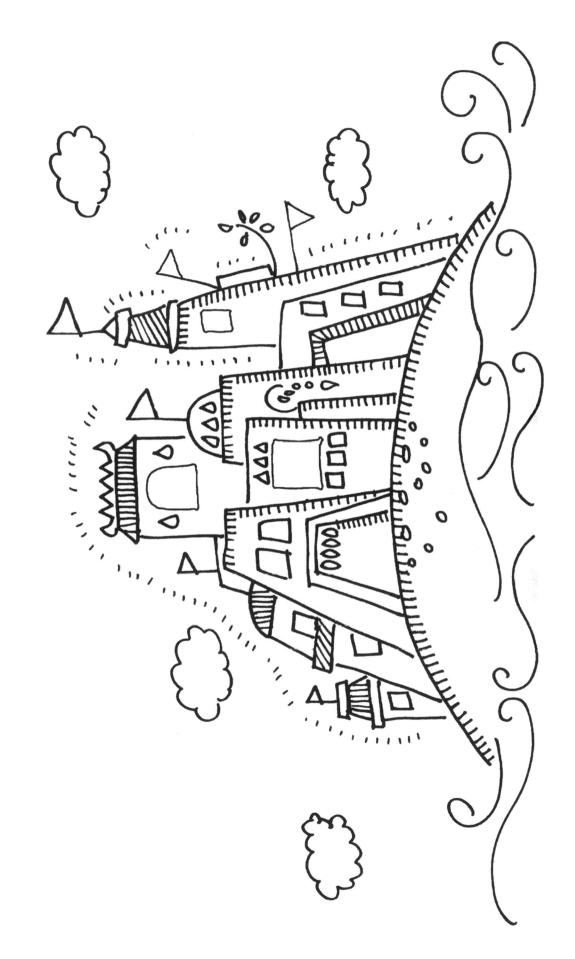

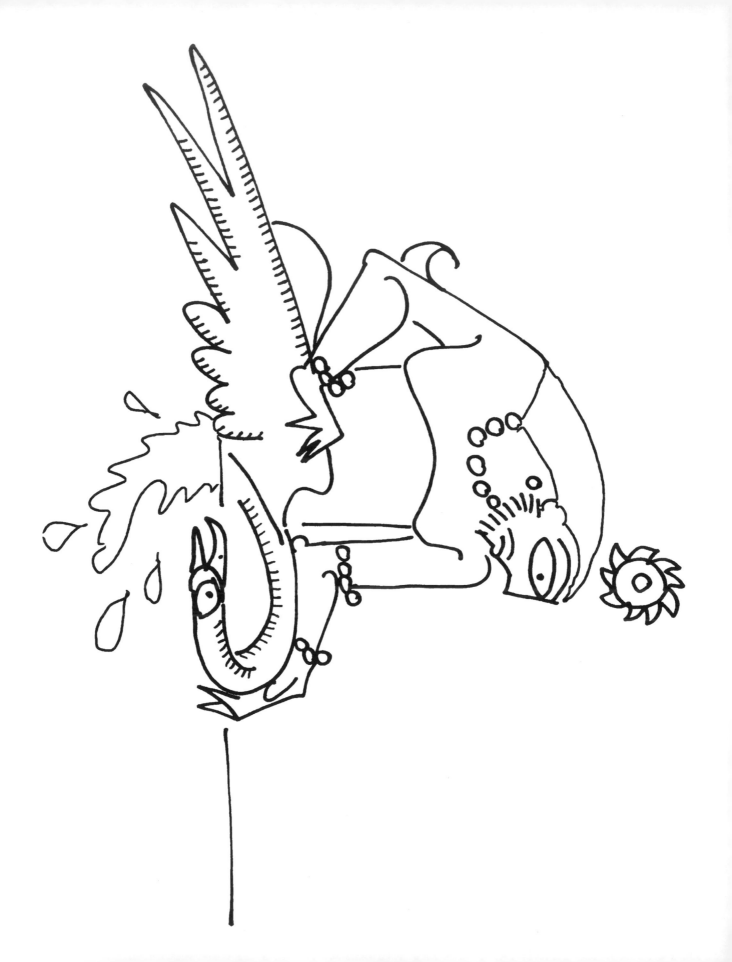

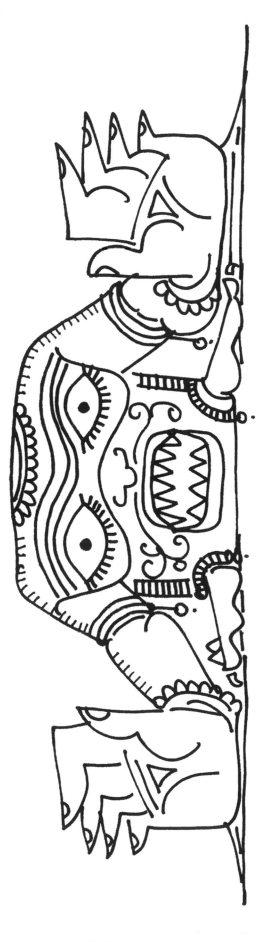

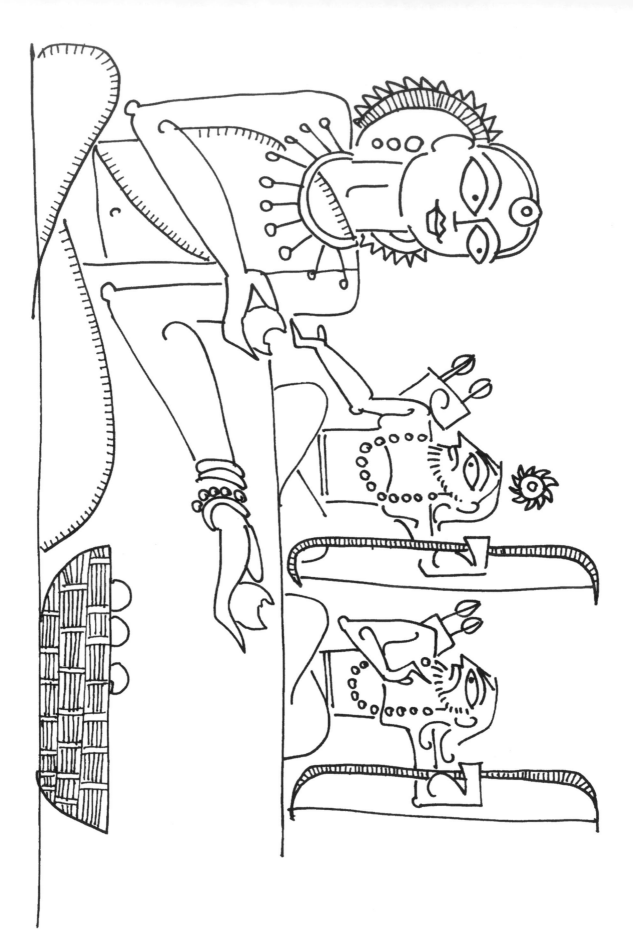

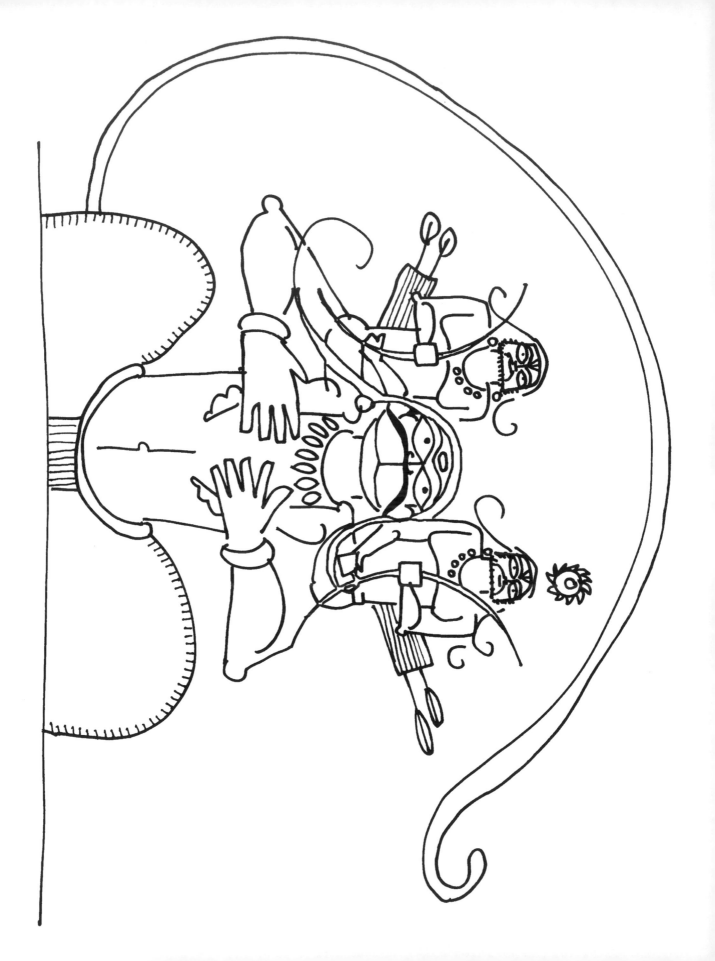

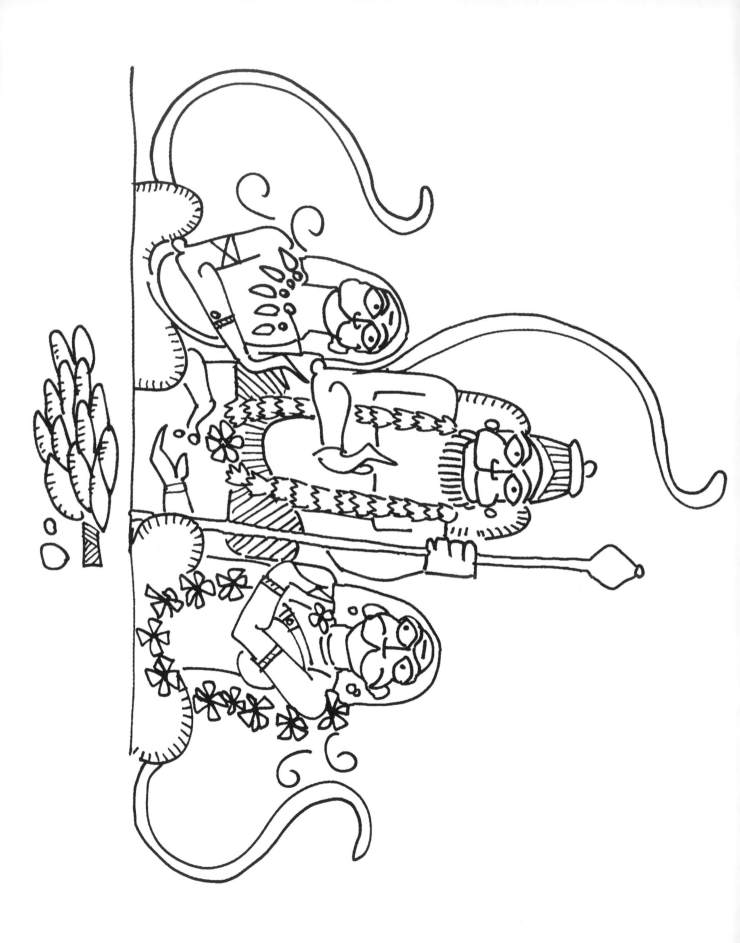

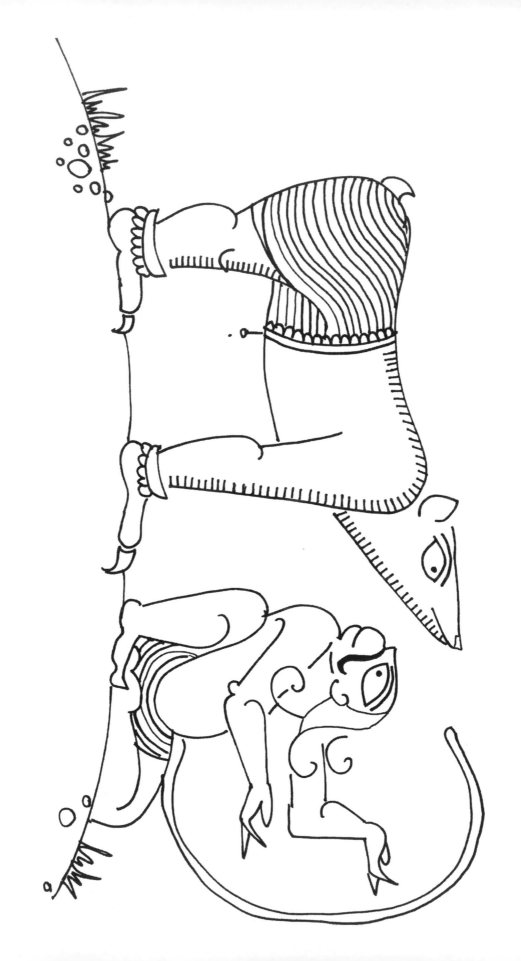

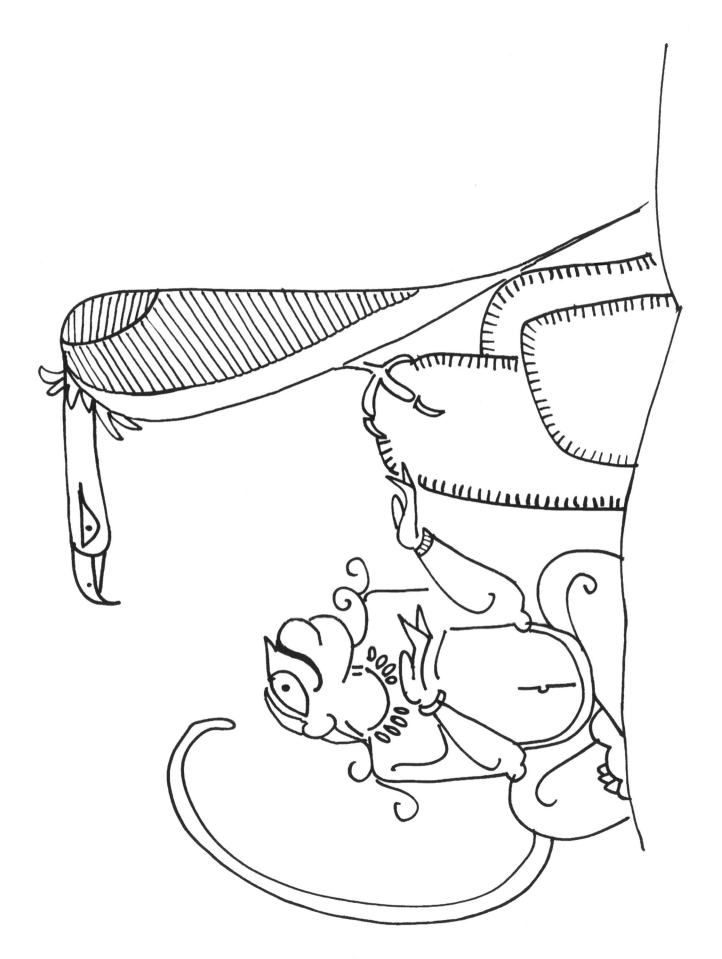

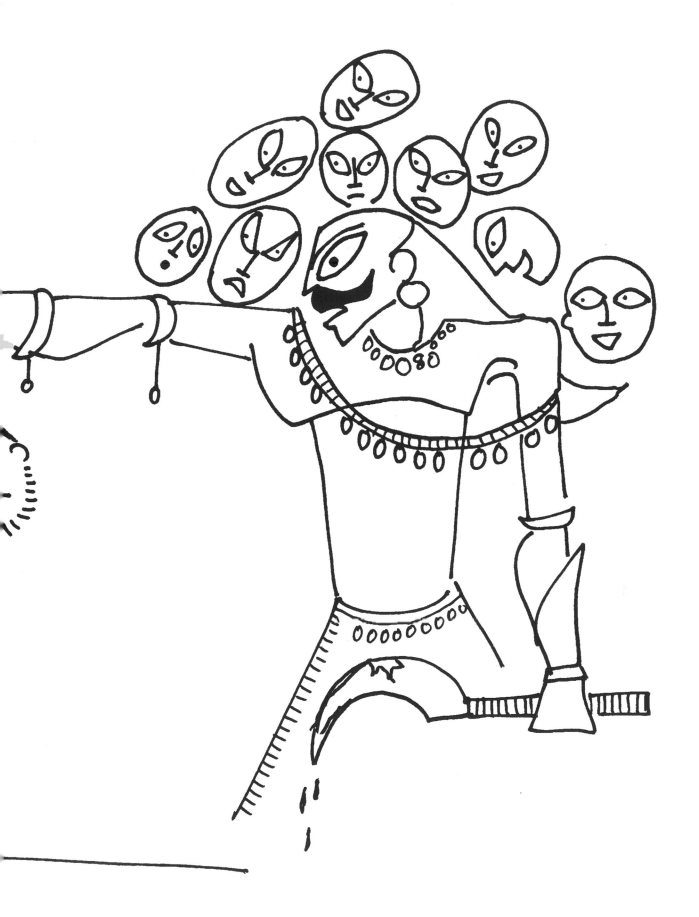

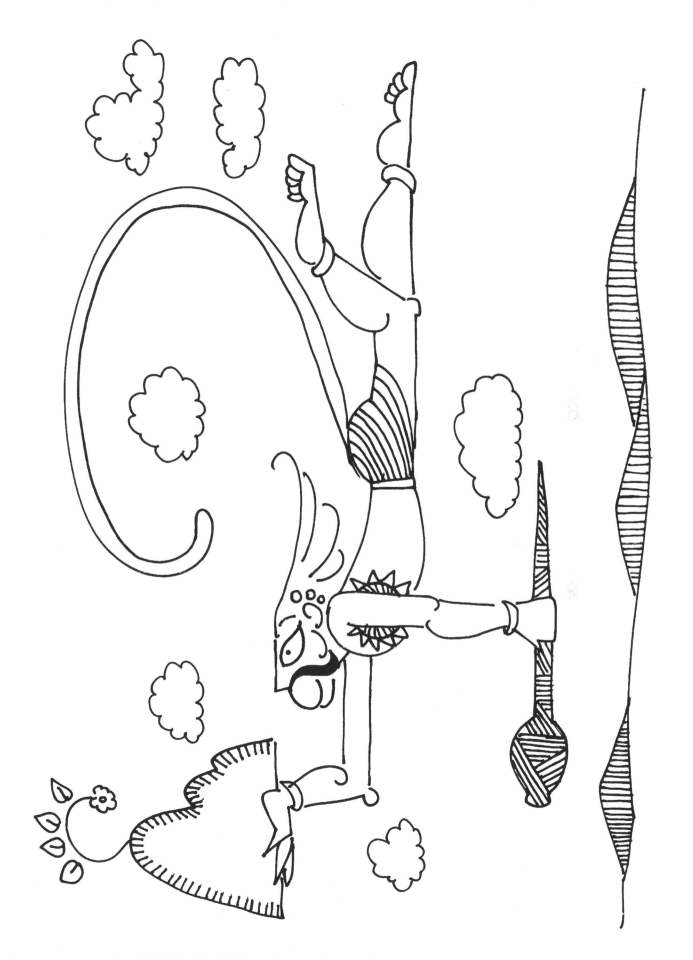

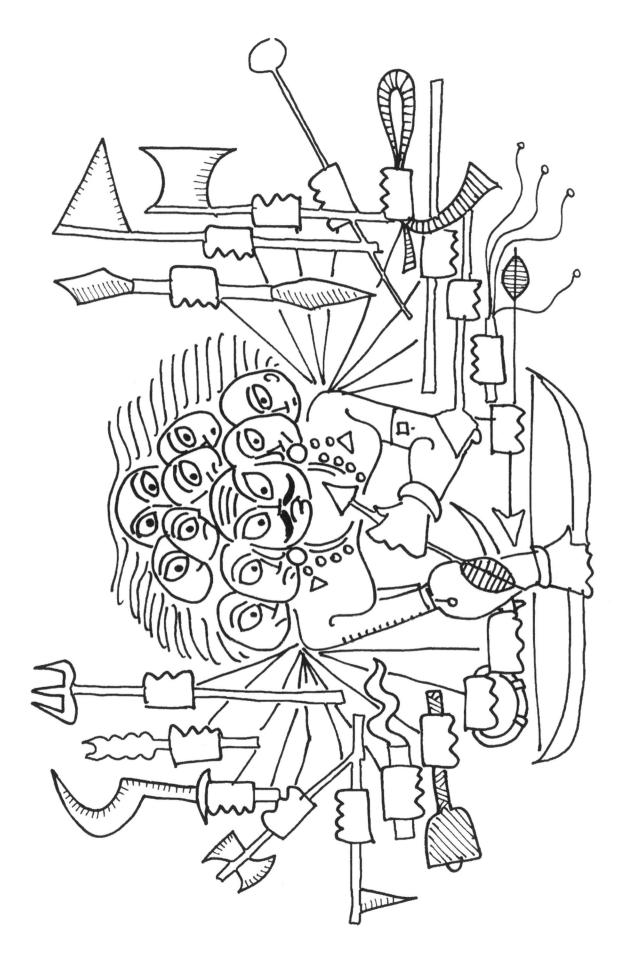

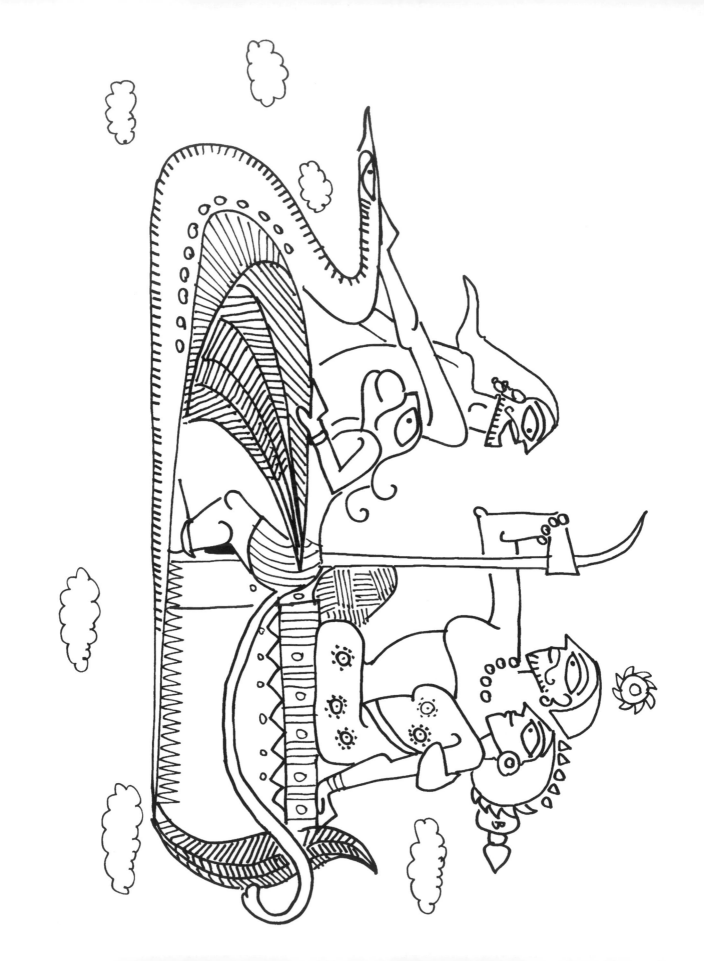

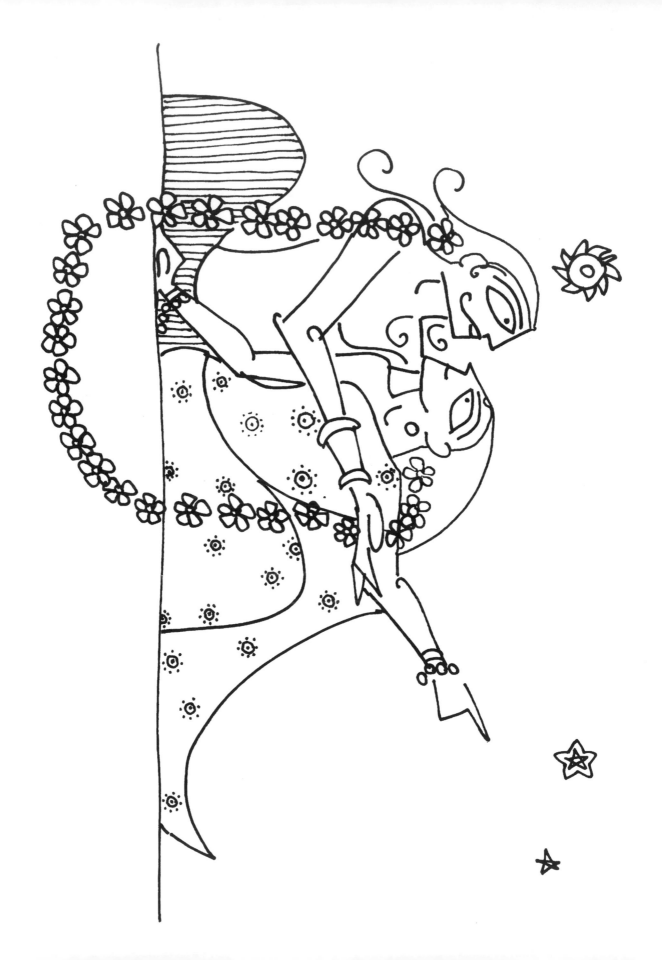

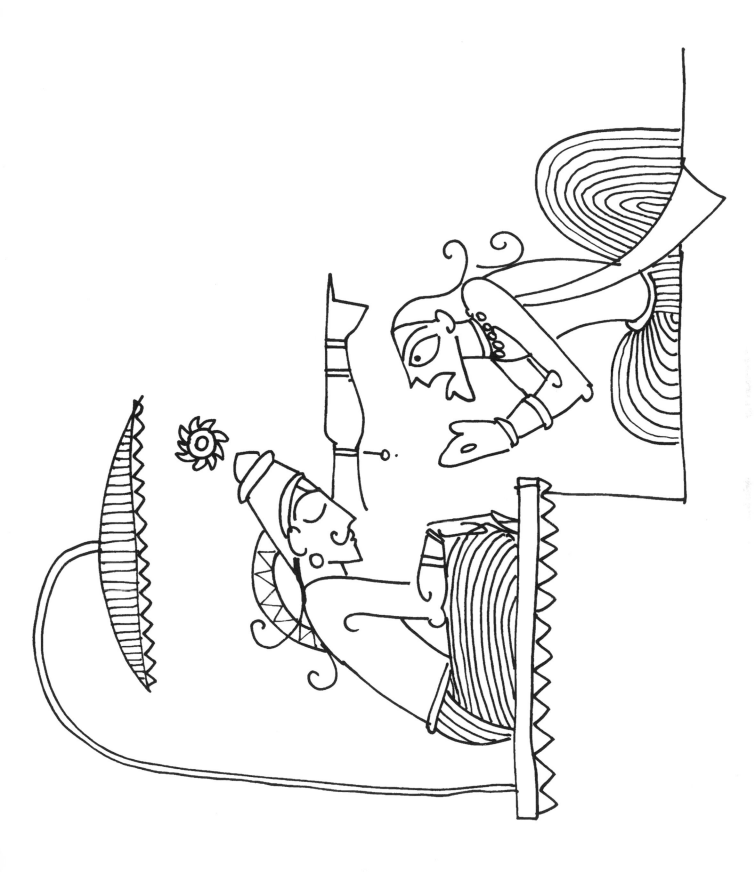

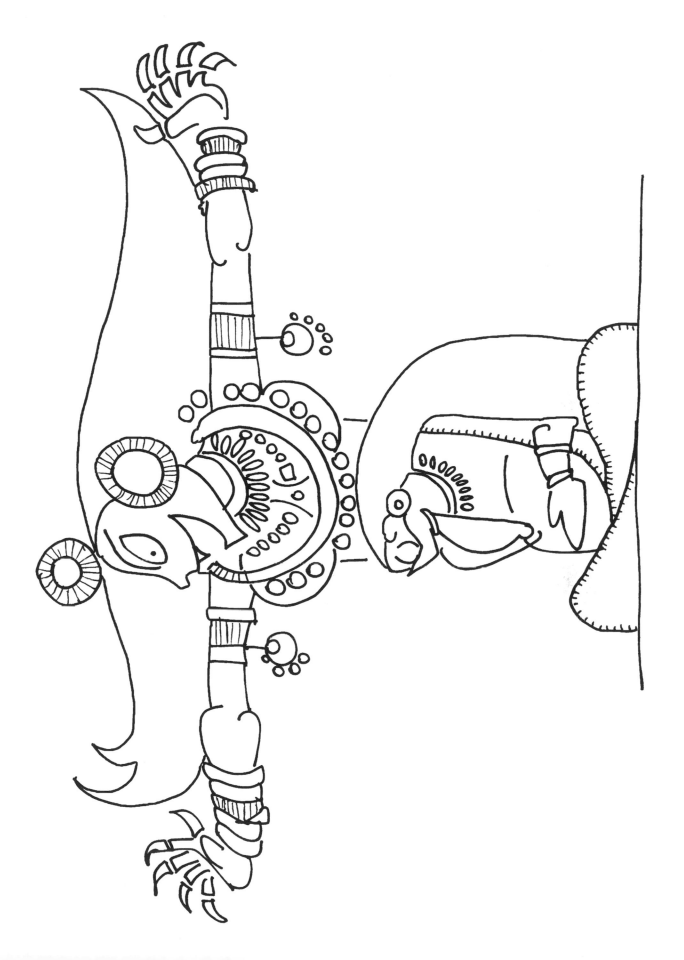

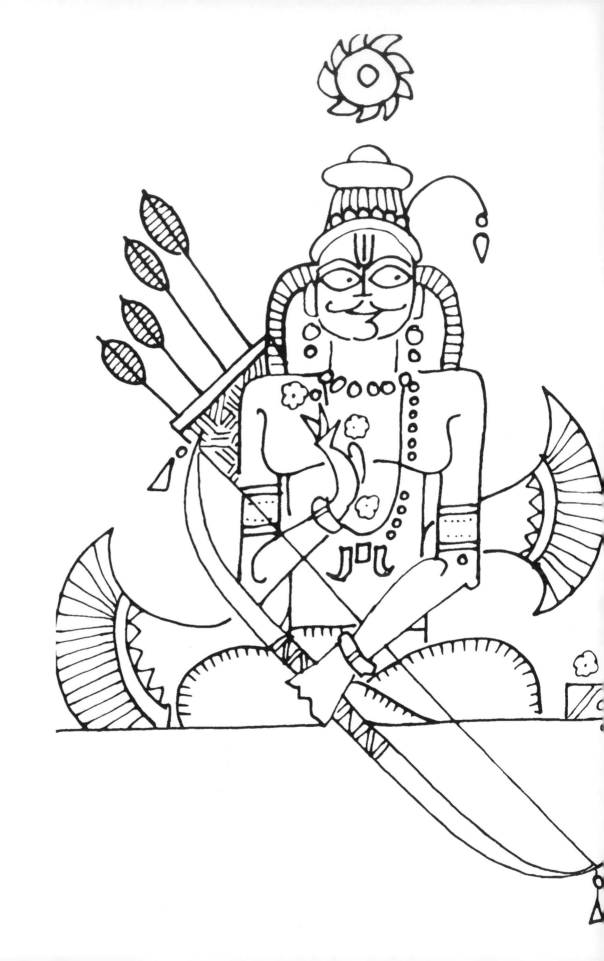

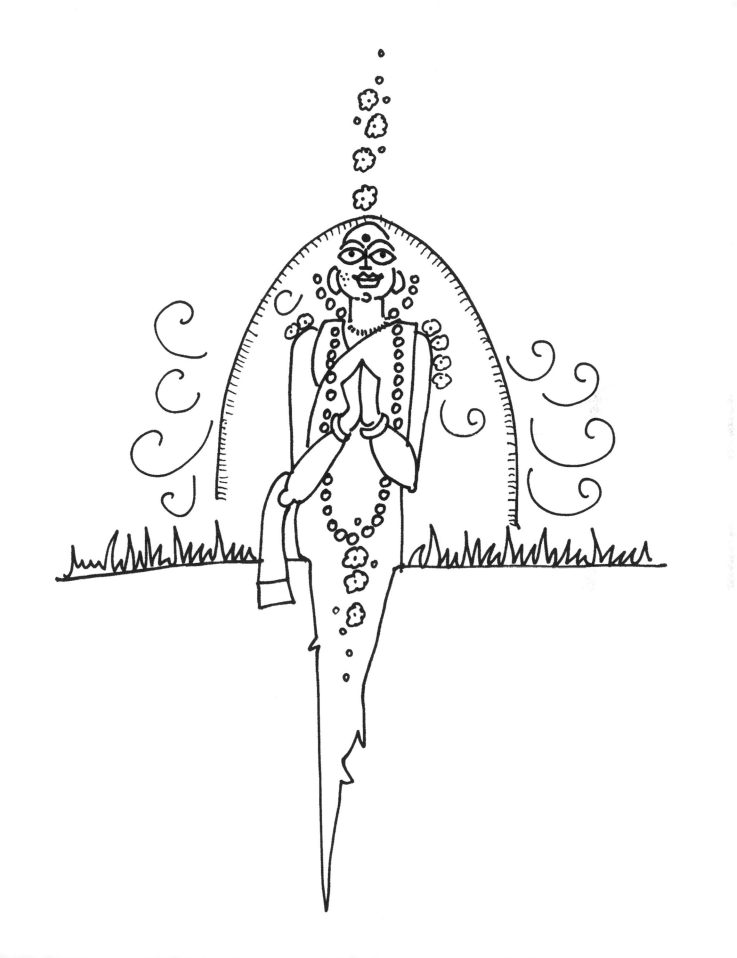

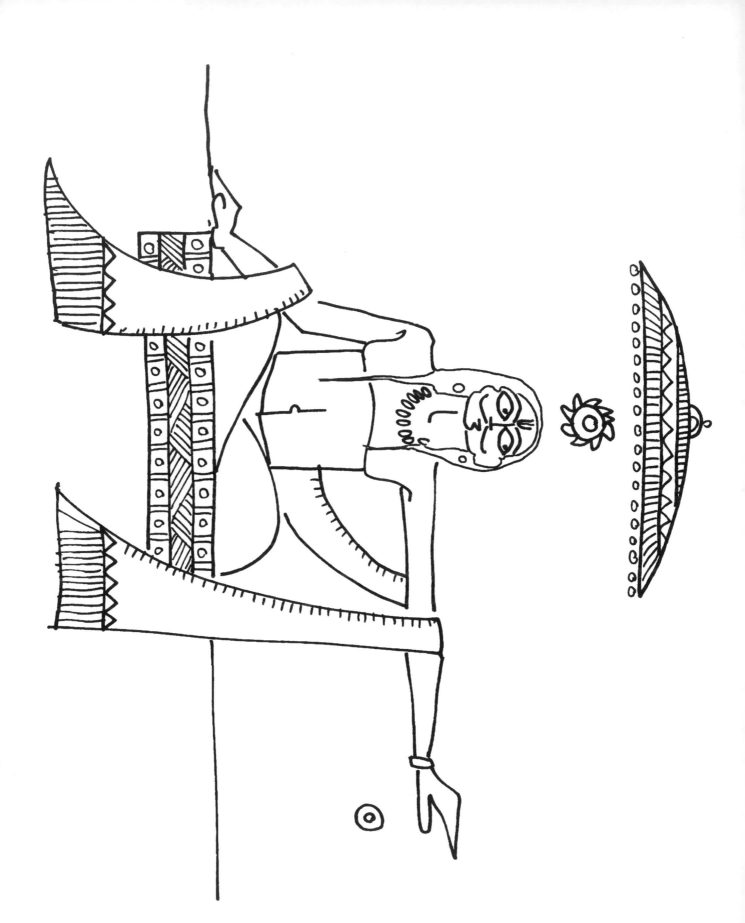

YOU MAY ALSO LIKE

Sita

Devdutt Pattanaik

It is significant that the only character in Hindu mythology, a king at that, to be given the title of *ekam-patni-vrata*, devoted to a single wife, is associated with the most unjust act of abandoning her in the forest to protect family reputation. This seems a deliberate souring of an uplifting narrative. Ram's refusal to remarry to produce a royal heir adds to the complexity. The intention seems to be to provoke thought on notions of fidelity, property and self-image.

And so mythologist and illustrator Devdutt Pattanaik retells the Ramayana, drawing attention to the many oral, visual and written retellings composed in different times, in different places, by different poets, each one trying to solve this puzzle in their own unique way.

This book approaches Ram by speculating on Sita: her childhood with her father, Janaka, who hosted sages mentioned in the Upanishads; her stay in the forest with her husband, who had to be a celibate ascetic while she was in the prime of her youth; her interactions with the women in Lanka, recipes she exchanged, emotions they shared; her connection with the earth, her mother, and the trees, her sisters; her role as the Goddess, the untamed Kali as well as the demure Gauri, in transforming the stoic prince of Ayodhya into God.

Penguin/PB

Jaya

Devdutt Pattanaik

High above the sky stands Swarga, paradise, abode of the gods. Still above is Vaikuntha, heaven, abode of God.
The doorkeepers of Vaikuntha are the twins, Jaya and Vijaya, both whose names mean 'victory'.
One keeps you in Swarga; the other raises you to Vaikuntha.
In Vaikuntha there is bliss forever, in Swarga there is pleasure for only as long as you deserve.
What is the difference between Jaya and Vijaya?
Solve this puzzle and you will solve the mystery of the Mahabharata.

In this enthralling retelling of India's greatest epic, the Mahabharata, originally known as Jaya, Devdutt Pattanaik seamlessly weaves into a single narrative plots from the Sanskrit classic as well as its many folk and regional variants, including the Pandavani of Chhattisgarh, Gondhal of Maharashtra, Terukkuttu of Tamil Nadu and Yakshagana of Kerala.

Richly illustrated with over 250 line drawings by the author, the 108 chapters abound with little known details such as the names of the hundred Kauravas, the worship of Draupadi as a goddess in Tamil Nadu, the stories of Astika, Madhavi, Jamini, Iravan and Barbareek, the Mahabharata version of the *Shakuntalam* and the Ramayana, and the dating of the war based on astronomical data.

With clarity and simplicity, the tales in this elegant volume reveal the external relevance of the Mahabharata, the complex and disturbing meditation on the human condition that has shaped Indian thought for over 3000 years.

Penguin/PB

The Jaya Colouring Book

Devdutt Pattanaik

Relive the great Indian epic the Mahabharata through 108 illustrations to be coloured in.

The Jaya Colouring Book, based on Devdutt Pattanaik's bestselling retelling of the Mahabharata, is a tremendous colouring adventure for you to embark on.

From the very beginning of the great epic (which Vyasa narrates as Ganesha writes the story down) till the dramatic end (when Yudhishtira is horrified to discover the Pandavas and Draupadi in Naraka), the entire story of the Mahabharata unfolds through Devdutt's inimitable illustrations.

Relive the drama of the greatest story ever told, from the birth of the Kauravas and Pandavas to Draupadi's swayamvara, the game of dice, the years in exile, and finally the great war of Kurukshetra.

Let your imagination run riot as you colour in the battle scenes—Krishna narrating the Bhagavad Gita to Arjuna, Bhima's slaying of Dusshasana and Duryodhana, and the deaths of Karna, Drona and Bhishma.

This is a great colouring adventure that readers of all ages will thoroughly enjoy.

Penguin/PB